Wellness Cove

Rosie   Alex   Bodhi   Izzy

Meet Your New Friends

This book belongs to:

_____

Grade:

_____

Introduction
Welcome To The Island Of Paradise Key

Welcome to the island of Paradise Key! You are about to begin an amazing wellness adventure where you will learn why it is important to take care of your mind and body. You will meet some great new friends on the island who will help guide you. Your first new friend is Coco the monkey. Coco is here to help you and will always be by your side on this journey.

Draw yourself here

New things can be scary, and that is normal. Luckily for you, Coco will be right by your side on this new adventure. First, draw a picture of yourself in the boat with Coco. **Also, as you journey through the workbook, color in the pages as you go.** Next, close your eyes and imagine that you are traveling to this new island. **What do you think you will see there? Why is it fun to use your imagination?**

Chapter 1
Meet The Kids On Paradise Key - Alex

On the dock next to you is Alex. He lives on a boat with his mom and dad. It is fun and exciting to live on a boat. However, Alex does not have a lot of friends because his family is always sailing from one island to the next. Alex's wishes that he had more friends.

Alex is **unique. Unique means different than everyone else.** Not many kids live on a boat! Like Alex, you are also unique. There is no one else exactly like you. It's a good thing that we are different, it makes life interesting. At home with your parents, or in school with your classmates, discuss the ways that you are unique or different from everyone else. **Try to come up with three things that make you unique.**

On the next 2 pages you will learn about the island of Paradise Key where you will begin your adventure.

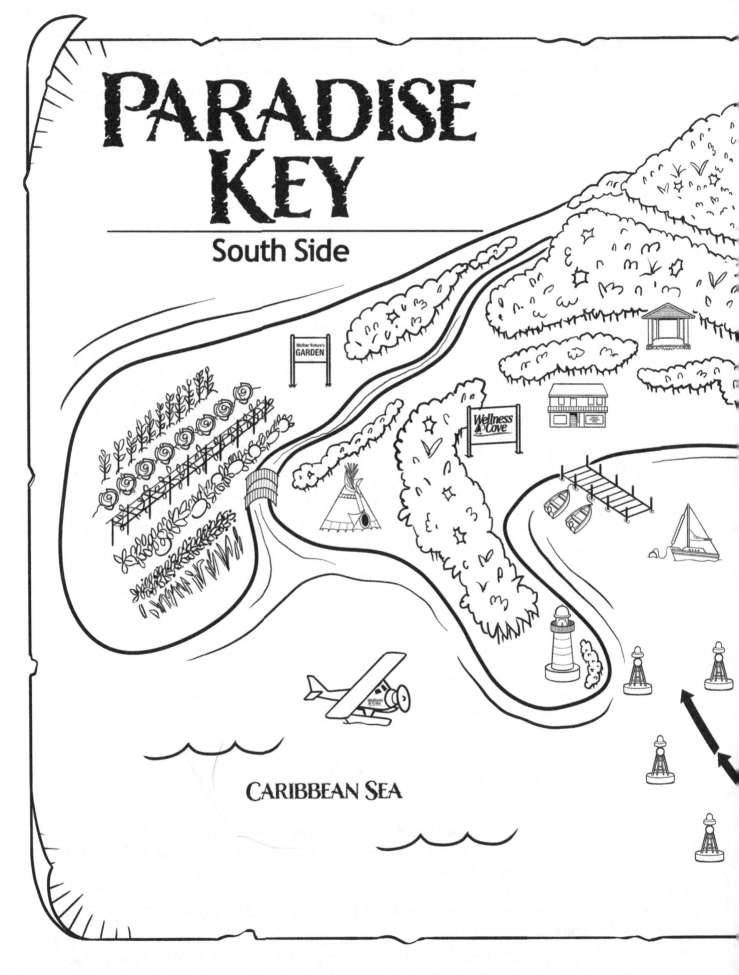

PARADISE KEY

South Side

Mother Nature's GARDEN

Wellness Cove

CARIBBEAN SEA

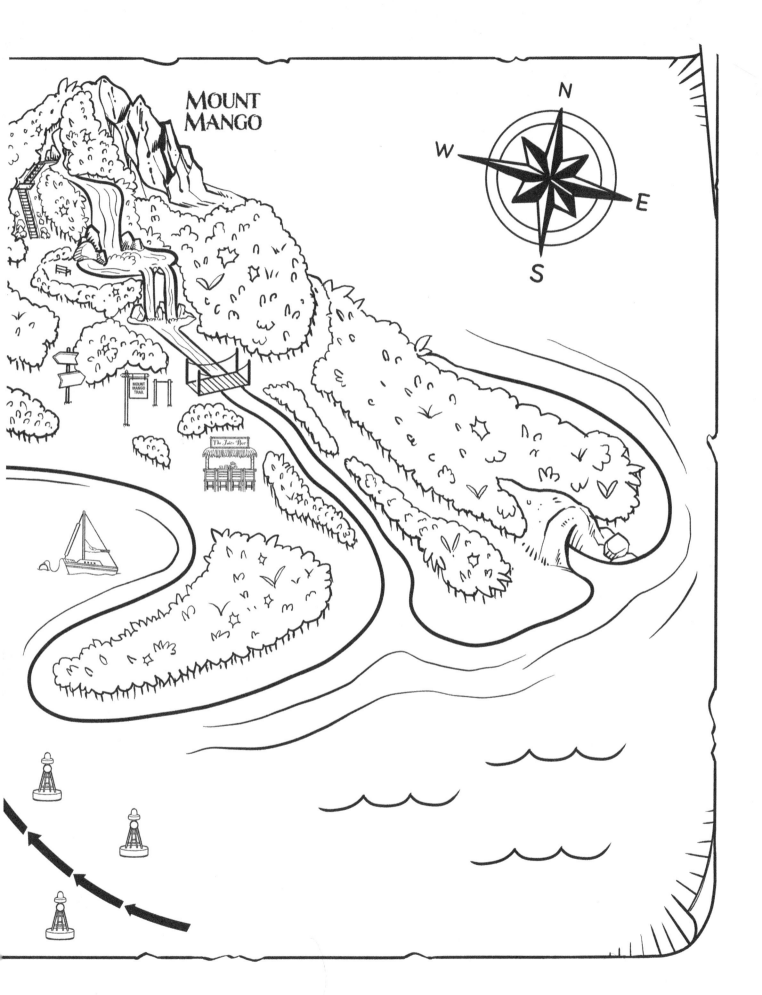

MOUNT
MANGO

5

Alex Goes In Search Of Fruit

One of the things that Alex loves to do each time he arrives at a new island is **to search for interesting fruits to eat.** This is called **foraging.** Here Coco is helping Alex pick some delicious bananas. Bananas are a special fruit because they give you a boost of energy to run fast or to play with your friends. Fruits, like the bananas here, fuel your body with the nutrients that it needs.

Try searching for interesting fruit to eat next time that you go to the store with your mom or dad. Can you find a banana? What other fruits did you find? What is a yellow fruit that gives you energy to run and play with your friends? Next time you are hungry for a snack, try a delicious banana or your favorite fruit. **How else can you get more fruits and vegetables into your diet?**

Rosie

Rosie lives on the other side of the island. She is very smart because she loves to read. There is a neat bookstore near her house where she likes to read. Rosie's favorite thing to read about is the ocean.

On page 4 and 5 of the workbook is a map of the island Paradise Key. Rosie loves to learn and she just finished reading a book about oceans. On page 4 and 5, color in the following things on the map: the ocean, the mountain, and the waterfall. Remember that the best way to learn is to ask questions. If you don't know the answer to something, ask for help. **Why do you want to become a good reader? What would you like to read about?**

Bodhi

Bodhi also lives on the other side of the island, but he lives on Banana Beach where he likes to surf every chance that he gets.

It's time to get some exercise. Let's go surfing with Bodhi! Play surfing music like Wipe Out by The Surfaris or Hawaii 5-0 by The Ventures. You can use an exercise balance board to surf and work on your balance. Bend your knees and keep your arms out like Bodhi. If this is unavailable, how else can you pretend to be surfing? As an alternative, you can dance to surfing music. Have your parent or teacher show you a video of "The Swim," a popular dance many years ago.

Izzy

Izzy lives in the forest far away from Banana Beach. Izzy loves the forest with all of the trees and birds. Her favorite thing to do is meditate. When you meditate, you try to just relax and think about breathing slowly. You try not to let your mind wander off, but if it does, that is fine, just try to come back to thinking about your breathing again.

Let's imagine that we are meditating with Izzy. It is best to play relaxing music or the sound of the ocean or a stream. Now, sit in a comfortable position. Place your hands on your knees or lap. Slowly close your eyes and then take three slow deep breaths. Keep your back tall like a mountain. Keep your hands, legs, and feet still like a mountain. Slowly breath in, and then slowly breath out. Do this for a few minutes, just focusing on your slow, deep breaths.

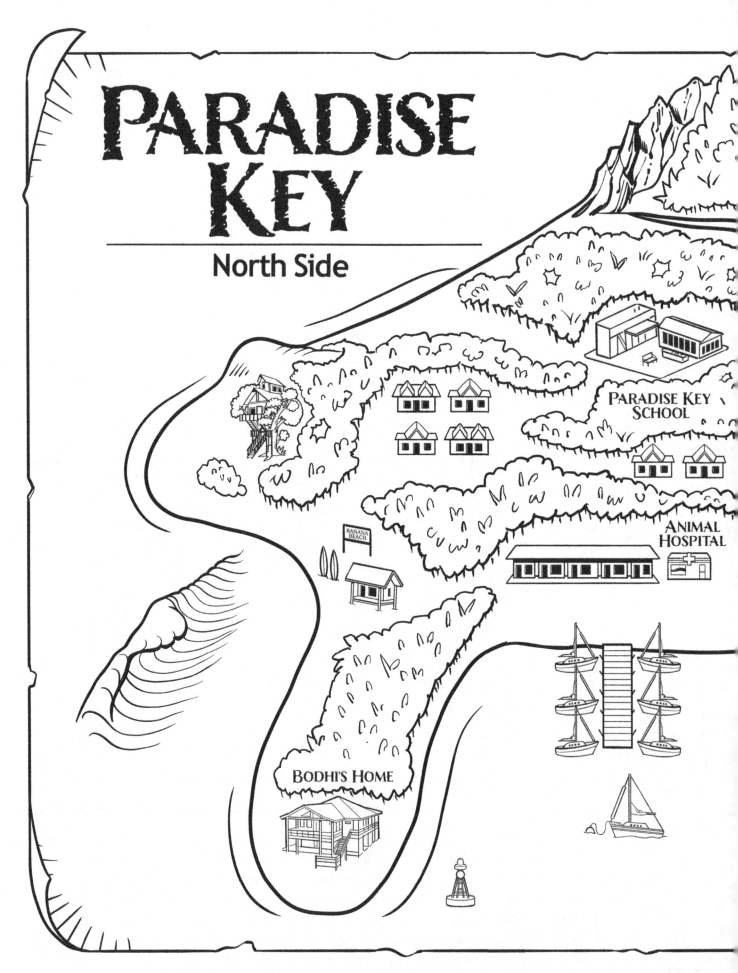

PARADISE KEY

North Side

PARADISE KEY SCHOOL

ANIMAL HOSPITAL

BANANA BEACH

BODHI'S HOME

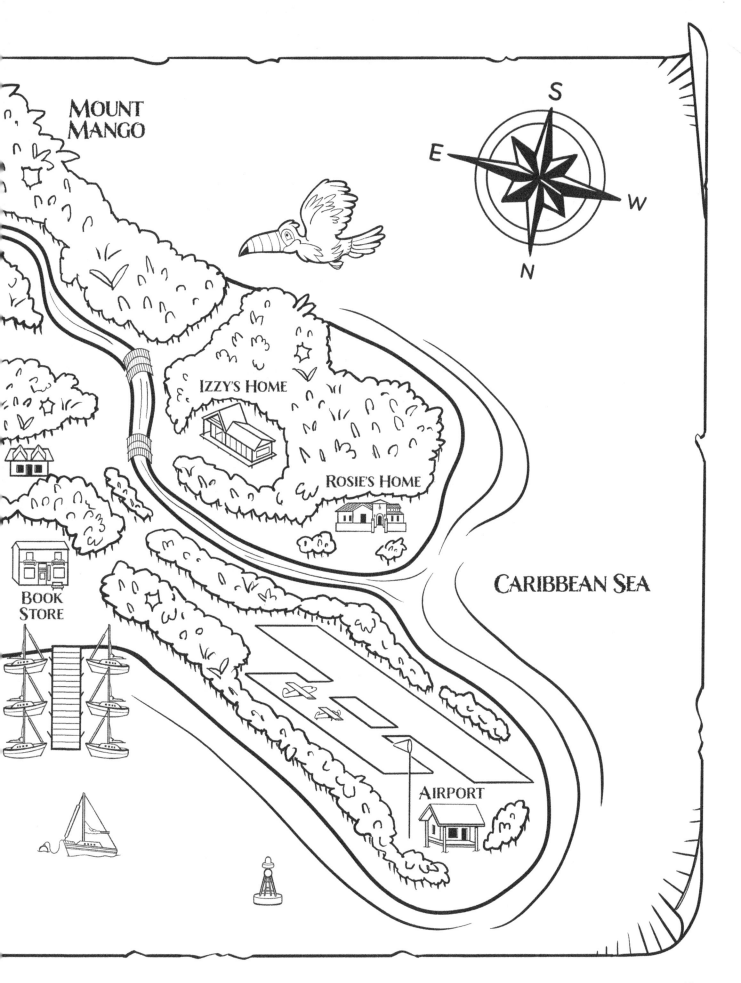

MOUNT MANGO

E S W N

IZZY'S HOME

ROSIE'S HOME

BOOK STORE

CARIBBEAN SEA

AIRPORT

11

Paradise Key School

Rosie, Bodhi, and Izzy all go to the same school, but they do not know each other. They sit in different parts of the classroom. Rosie likes learning and enjoys school, but Bodhi and Izzy have a hard time in school. Bodhi would rather be surfing, and Izzy is shy and has a hard time meeting new friends.

You know a little bit about Alex, Rosie, Bodhi, and Izzy. Let's learn a little bit about you. In the space to the right draw something that you like to do. After you are done, your teacher may ask you to share what you drew. It is pretty cool that we are all different and that makes life fun.

Homeschool

Alex does not go to school with the other kids because he is homeschooled. **Homeschool is when your parents teach you at home instead of going to school.** If you are homeschooled, it is important to make friends outside of school. However, this is hard for Alex because his family is always sailing to different islands. Alex wishes that he could just stay on one island, but he is afraid to tell his parents. After all, he is "just a kid."

Alex treasures his family. **To treasure something means to treat it as something very special and important.** See if you can find and color in the 3 treasure chests hidden on this page. Also find Coco and color him in. Tonight, enjoy eating dinner with your family and talking with them. It is fun to be with your family because they will always be by your side. **What is your favorite thing about your family?**

Chapter 2

Fate Brings The Kids Together

Color in the blueberries blue or purple.

I wish that I had kids my age to hang out with.

Let's try to eat a blueberry **mindfully. To eat mindfully means to slow down and really pay attention to what you are eating.** First, look at the blueberry. What color is it? Smell it. Feel it. Is it big or small? Then, slowly eat it. What does it taste like? Is it sweet and delicious? Know that blueberries are full of nutrients that are healthy for your brain. **Why is it important to eat mindfully?**

Rosie Reads On The Beach

Rosie loves to read on the beach. She has been reading a lot about the ocean lately. Her brain is filled with lots of interesting facts about animals because she is always reading and learning.

dolphin   flying fish   turtle   seagull

Trace the letters of all the animals in Rosie's book. When you trace these letters you are learning and making your brain stronger. **What is something that you would love to read and learn about?**

15

Bodhi Goes For A Bike Ride

Not only does Bodhi surf, but he does lots of other kinds of **exercise. Exercise is when you move your body in order to make it stronger.** Biking, walking, and swimming are all examples of exercise. When you get outside and exercise, you can enjoy our amazing planet. Bodhi is enjoying all of the cool wildlife on Mount Mango.

Draw your favorite exercise here.

If you have a bike, go for a bike ride today. Pretend that you are riding with Bodhi! Be sure to wear your helmet. Biking is a great way to move your body and get some exercise. If you do not have a bike, how else could you move your body today? In the space to the right, draw your favorite way to exercise.

EXERCISE BREAK

Izzy Finds A Cool Spot To Do Yoga

Izzy loves to walk in the forest. On her walk, she finds a cool spot where she can do yoga. Yoga is a type of exercise in which you try to hold different positions with your body. Just like with meditation, in yoga, you focus on your breathing and relaxing your body. Yoga is a great way to stretch and strengthen your muscles to make you stronger.

Let's do some yoga with Izzy. Stand behind your desk and try to hold each of the yoga poses above for 5 seconds. Color in each pose! **Why do you think yoga is good for your body? Why might it also be good for your brain?**

Mother Nature

While Alex, Rosie, Bodhi, and Izzy are all out enjoying our amazing planet, a bad rainstorm comes out of nowhere. All 4 of the kids run for shelter! They all end up near a large teepee in an open field. Standing at the entrance is an elderly woman with a big smile. Her name is Mother Nature. She motions them to come in so that they can find shelter from the storm.

Next time it rains, try one of these options or come up with one of your own.

1. Do some creative dancing. Creative dancing is when you move your body in a fun and creative way to music.

2. Try to stretch every muscle in your body. Think about what muscle you are stretching and try to feel the stretch.

Why is it important to move your body every day, even if it rains?

Wellness

Mother Nature helps the kids warm up by serving them hot coco inside her teepee. She tells the kids that she has been watching them and they seem to know a lot about **wellness. Wellness is taking care of your brain and body.** Mother Nature observes that Alex knows to eat healthy fruits and vegetables. Izzy takes care of her brain and body by relaxing each day. Bodhi takes care of his body by surfing and exercising. And Rosie, exercises her brain by reading so much.

Our symbol for wellness is a sailboat because wellness is a journey. Wellness is something that you work on for your entire life. You are now beginning that exciting adventure! Find the 5 hearts hidden outside the teepee. Each heart has a wellness secret inside. Find all 5 hearts and outline them with red. **What is your wellness secret? Why is it important to take care of your brain and your body?**

After The Storm

After the rainstorm passes Mother Nature walks the kids home. They come across a beautiful rainbow. They stop to enjoy the beautiful colors and the nature around them. It is important to stop and enjoy our beautiful planet each and every day, even if it is simply looking up at the clouds. It is important to take care of our planet. When we take care of our planet it makes Mother Nature happy.

Color in the beautiful rainbow. Next color the flowers on the bottom of the page using the same colors as the rainbow. Finally, go outside and enjoy this beautiful planet! Find one thing you noticed that was beautiful outside and draw it in the cloud above. **Why is it important to enjoy our beautiful planet?**

Shinrin Yoku

First, Mother Nature takes Izzy home. Outside of her house, Izzy's grandfather is doing **Shinrin Yoku. Shinrin Yoku is when you quietly walk through a forest and observe what you see, hear, feel, and smell.** Shinrin Yoku is healthy for your body and brain. It also helps you become a better scientist because you become a good observer. It even helps you stay focused more in school.

Trace Words

Let's practice Shinrin Yoku. Go outside for 10 minutes and quietly walk around, observing all the nature around you. In the spaces below, write or draw what you saw, heard, felt, and smelled.

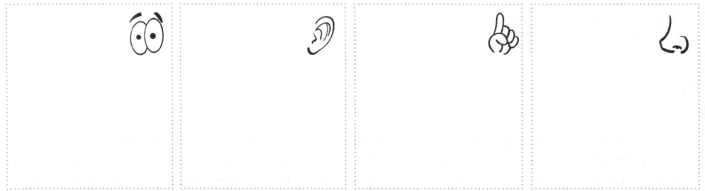

A Love For Reading

Next, Mother Nature drops off Rosie at her mother's office. Rosie got her love of reading from her mom. Rosie's mom is a Veterinarian and is always reading about animals. At first, Rosie had a hard time learning to read. Her mom told her that the more she practiced reading the stronger she was making her brain. Rosie kept practicing and strengthening her brain and she began to read easily. Rosie finds that reading relaxes her body and calms her mind. Her favorite thing to read about is the ocean and ways to protect it.

Lets strengthen your brain right now. There are 5 brains hidden on this page. See if you can find them all. In order to make your brain strong, read tonight for 10 minutes with one of your parents. Then get a good night's sleep. That is also good for your brain! **Why do you think reading is good for your brain? What could you read tonight? Why do you think sleep is good for your brain?**

Helping Others

Next, Mother Nature takes Bodhi home. Bodhi's house is right on Banana Beach which makes it easy for him to go surfing every day. His parents are known around the island for always doing nice things for other people.

It's time to get some exercise. When you use your muscles, you get stronger. This allows you to do harder things like climb and jump. To the right Bodhi is planking. Planking requires you to use your stomach muscles. Let's see how strong your stomach is. See how long you can plank.

Alex Seems Sad

Finally, Mother Nature takes Alex home. She notices that Alex is quiet and seems sad. As they talk, Alex explains that it is hard to make friends because every time he makes a new friend, his family sails off to another island. Mother Nature asks Alex, "Have you ever talked to your parents about this?" Alex responds, "I'm afraid to tell them. I'm just a kid."

Your parents love you and will always want to help you. They never want you to be sad. When you have a problem it is always best to talk to your parents. Try to spend time talking with your mom and dad when you get home from school. When your parents ask you what you did today, tell them the best thing about your day. Ask your parents or teacher about their day.

Chapter 3
The Wellness Crew

Rosie, Bodhi, and Izzy are now friends at school. Since Alex does homeschooling he does not go to school with them. However, they ask Alex to hang out with them after school the next day. Alex explains to the others that he will probably have to leave the island soon because his parents usually only stay at one island for a few weeks.

Hanging out with friends is healthy. Not only can you laugh and have fun, but it is nice to have someone to talk to when you are sad. Try to learn more about your friends next time that you are hanging out together. When your friends are talking, try to be a good listener. **Why is it important to have friends? Why is it important to be kind to your friends?**

Mr. Bob

The next day Alex, Izzy, Bodhi, and Rosie are hiking on Mount Mango. They meet another friendly hiker. Rosie recognizes him because he is the bookshop owner, Mr. Bob. Mr. Bob notices that the kids seem very happy and healthy. He comes up with a great idea. If they can come up with their secrets to being happy and healthy, he will print a book for them so that they can share their secrets with other kids.

Draw yourself here

Mr. Bob likes to hike and enjoy our amazing planet. At recess, or when you go home today, enjoy the outdoors. Use all of your senses. What do you see? What do you smell? What do you hear? What do things feel like? Can you find the most beautiful tree or plant? What animals or birds can you find? **Why is it important to be grateful for all the beautiful plants and animals outside? What does it mean to be grateful?**

Coming Up With A Plan

The Wellness Crew get together to come up with their secrets for living a happy and healthy life. Rosie has volunteered to write down their ideas in a notebook. Each of the kids in the Wellness Crew have great ideas about how to be happy and healthy. For example, Alex knows a lot about eating healthy.

Alex picked some raspberries for the kids to snack on. Fruits like raspberries are loaded with vitamins and minerals that your body needs . Alex feels good about himself because he knows that he is needed. The other kids respect his knowledge about healthy eating. The next time that you go to the store with your mom or dad, ask them to buy raspberries, or choose another fruit to try. Tell your parents why fruits are healthy. You can even teach them how to eat mindfully. **What does it mean to eat mindfully?**

Mother Nature Helps Out

The Wellness Crew needs to come up with their secrets to Wellness. They are not quite sure where to start. They decide to ask Mother Nature for some help. She explains that Wellness is all about being happy and healthy. She explains that In order to be happy, the most important thing is to know that you are loved. There is no one else on the planet exactly like you. God created you, and loves you, just the way you are.

Whenever you see a rainbow, know that God loves you.

Draw yourself here

In the hearts to the right, draw something you love about yourself and something you love about one of your friends. At home draw a rainbow and tape it next to your bed so that when you wake up each morning, and before you go to bed each night, you will be reminded that God loves you.

Love Yourself - Love Others

In addition to loving yourself just as you are, Mother Nature explains to the Wellness Crew how important it is to love others just as they are. We should never change who we are to try to please others. True friends will love you just as you are. The Wellness Crew are all very different, yet they still love each other. They decide to make "Love yourself and Love Others," their first wellness secret.

Think of ways to show your family that you really love them. How can you show your friends that you really care about them? Finally, what are ways that you can be kind to yourself?

Do one of the following today or come up with an idea of your own.

Below are 3 examples of how to love yourself or love others.

- Ask your mom or dad how their day was.
- Listen to your friend if they have a problem that they want to talk about.
- If you make a mistake, realize that we all make mistakes and just try to learn from it.

Move Your Body

The next day, the Wellness Crew continue to work on their Wellness Secrets. Bodhi starts off by saying that his secret to being well is to exercise and move his body. Bodhi exercises by surfing on the beautiful ocean and biking on cool trails in the woods. Alex gets exercise by foraging in order to find healthy foods. Izzy exercises by doing yoga by the waterfall near her house. Rosie exercises by walking to the beach to read. They all like to exercise outside so that they can enjoy this amazing planet.

The Wellness Crew have their own favorite way to exercise and move their bodies. In the box above, draw your favorite way to exercise or move your body. See if you can do one of the exercises from above today. **Why do you think exercising every day is healthy?**

A Long Swim

Later that day, the Wellness Crew decide to swim out to Alex's sailboat to watch the sunset. They all agree that it is really fun to be outside doing fun stuff. By being healthy they are able to do things like this and enjoy this amazing planet. The Wellness Crew decides to make "Enjoy this Amazing Planet" their 2nd secret to living a happy, healthy life.

Draw yourself here

Let's get outside and enjoy this amazing planet. You can hike, bike, shoot hoops, kick the soccer ball, whatever you want, but do it outdoors. Breath in the fresh air, take in the beauty of the outdoors, and enjoy this amazing planet! **What is the most beautiful thing you saw outside today?**

A Beautiful Sunset

The Wellness Crew catches a sunset on Alex's boat. They all agree that taking time to just relax every day is super important. It gives your body and brain a chance to rest. That's why Izzy meditates every day. She realizes how important this is for her wellness. She suggests that they make "Chill Every Day" their 3rd wellness secret.

When you meditate, you can pretend that you are anywhere in the world! Let's meditate and imagine that we are hanging out out on Alex's boat with the Wellness Crew. Sit in a comfortable position. Place your hands on your knees or lap. Slowly close your eyes and then take 3 slow deep breaths. Keep your back tall like a mountain. Now join the Wellness Crew on Alex's boat. Just chill with them for a few minutes. **How did you feel after you meditated?**

A Beautiful Day For Sailing

The following day, Alex's parents take the Wellness Crew out sailing. On their way back into the cove, Alex's dad explains the purpose of the lighthouse, the buoys, and the cove where the boat will be protected and safe.

#4 It's Cool To Be Smart

Cove
A protected area of an island where boats can be sheltered from storms.

Lighthouse
Tall structures with a bright light at the top to help guide boats to safety during a storm.

Buoy
Keeps boats away from rocks and other dangerous objects. There are 7 Buoys that guide boats into the cove on Paradise Key.

The Wellness Crew thought that it was really fun to learn about the purpose of lighthouses, buoys, and coves. Rosie says, "I told you that it's fun to learn and cool to be smart!" Rosie thinks that this should be their 4th secret to living a happy and healthy life. See if your parents can help you find pictures of interesting lighthouses on their computer. Explain to them why boats depend upon lighthouses during a storm. If you want, you can draw your favorite lighthouse and bring it in to show your teacher.

Mother Nature's Garden

The next day, the Wellness Crew visits Mother Nature. She is out working in her garden. Alex is impressed with all of the different fruits and vegetables that she is growing. Alex says, "Wow, that is Mother Nature's secret to living such a long and healthy life. That should be our 5th wellness secret, "fuel your body with the nutrients that it needs." Alex's knows that fruits and vegetables have all of the vitamins, and nutrients that your body needs.

Try having a fruit or vegetable as your snack today. That way you will be eating out of Mother Nature's garden instead of eating packaged food that may not be as healthy for you. **How can you get more fruits and vegetables into your diet?**

Hara Hachi Bu

From Mother Nature's Garden the kids hike to Izzy's house for lunch. Izzy's Mother teaches them the Japanese tradition of Hara Hachi Bu . In Japan, many families say "hara hachi bu" before each meal in order to remind them to stop eating before they are completely full.

Draw yourself here

Try doing Hara Hachi Bu for lunch or dinner today. Eat your food slowly. Enjoy the taste and the smell of the food. Enjoy the people that you're with. Notice when you start to get full. Try to stop eating before you are too full. **Why is it healthy to stop eating when you are full?**

Pirate Alert!

A pirate ship is often seen around the island. The Wellness Crew like to keep an eye on the ship. Here Rosie spotted them eating too much junk food. Too much junk food like soft drinks, candy, and chips can make you tired and not feel so well.

Try to set an example for the pirates by drinking water instead of sugary soft drinks. See if you can drink 3 glasses of water today. **Why is water healthier than sugary soft drinks?**

Rosie's Dad

Rosie's dad builds surfboards for a living. He works out of his garage. Rosie likes hanging out with her dad when he is working because he makes her laugh. Rosie tells him about her new friends including Bodhi who surfs. Her dad says that he has heard about Bodhi.

Spend some time with your family tonight. See if you can make them laugh. Laughter is very healthy. It helps you feel good and makes you happy. It even helps you stay healthy and avoid getting sick. **How can you make your family laugh? Why do you think that laughing is healthy?**

Family Is Everything

The Wellness Crew is enjoying a healthy snack that they bought at the Provisions Store in the Cove. Rosie tells the others how much she enjoys hanging out with her parents. All of the kids agree that they have great parents. Rosie suggests that Treasure Your Family should be one of their wellness secrets. All of the kids agree.

Alex's mom notices that Alex is really having fun with his new friends. She worries that Alex will miss his friends when they leave the island. Likewise, Alex is sad that he will be leaving soon. **On the lines below write down what you think Alex should do so that his family will stay on Paradise Key instead of leaving.**

_____

— —

_____

The Secret To Happiness

The Wellness Crew hike all the way to the top of Mount Mango. They all think that something is missing from their secrets to living a happy and healthy life. Bodhi tells his friends "My dad is always telling me that the secret to being happy is to help others. Alex adds, " and to help our planet." Izzy thinks that their final secret to happiness is to " Help others and help the planet."

When you use your talents to help others and to help the planet, it makes you feel happy and proud. Look for some cloths or toys at home that you could donate to charity for another child. Ask your parents to take your gifts to a local charity like Goodwill or Salvation Army. **How does it make you feel to help others? How else could you help others or help the planet?**

The 7 Secrets To Wellness

The Wellness Crew discovered a room above the Provisions Store that is filled with books and maps. They also find an old chalkboard and decide to write down their 7 secrets to Wellness. Remember wellness means taking care of your brain and body. To be well means that you are happy and healthy. The kids do not like the term secrets, because they don't want them to be secrets. They want to share them with all children so that they can all live happy and healthy lives.

The Wellness Crew wants to share these 7 guiding secrets with other children. **Who could you share these principles with? Would these guiding principles be good for adults to know?** Share your knowledge about wellness with someone else. You could even share them with your parents.

A Name For Their Book!

Next to the chalkboard, Alex finds a map of the south side of Paradise Key. It shows 7 buoys leading into the cove where boats can find protection from storms. Bodhi points out that the 7 Buoys keep you on the correct path to the cove where it is peaceful. Alex, has a great idea, "Let's write our 7 secrets to wellness on each of the 7 buoys. Then, they will not be secrets and everyone who comes to our island can learn them.

That would be a great name for our book! The 7 Buoys!

Alex came up with a great name for their book, *The 7 Buoys*. Alex has contributed a lot to the book and the Wellness Crew is sad that he might be leaving the island soon. Sometimes when you are sad it helps to get outside and get some exercise. You can go for a walk, play soccer with your friends, or maybe do some Shinrin Yoku like you did on page 22. Go outside and get some exercise at recess or when you get home from school. Exercise and fresh air will make you happy, and that is what wellness is all about.

Chapter 4
Alex Faces His Fears

Alex knows that he will have to leave the island of Paradise Key soon. He is sad because he has made such good friends and feels like he is part of the Wellness Crew. As he is walking with Coco, he notices a brave squirrel jumping from one tree to another. This gives him an idea! He thinks, "I need to have courage like that squirrel and talk to my parents." When you have courage you are able to do something even when you are afraid. Alex names the brave squirrel "Sammy."

The lion is a symbol of courage. See if you can find the Lion hidden on this page. Let's try to be courageous like a lion. Try something that you are a little afraid to do. Here are some examples, play soccer or basketball with your friends even if you are not really that good at it. You may be better than you think. Another example, would be to eat lunch with some kids that you don't really know that well. Maybe you will find that you have more in common with them than you think. **How else could you be courageous?**

Alex Talks To His Parents

Alex gets up the courage to tell his parents that he really wants to stay on Paradise Key with his new friends. He explains to them that he feels good about himself because he is part of the Wellness Crew, and they need him. His parents understand and they also really like the island. However, Alex's dad explains that he would have to rent a place to dock the boat and that can be expensive. Alex's parents would be willing to stay if he could find a job to pay for the dock slip.

Alex's parents are both good listeners. Because they take the time to listen to Alex, they now understand him better and want to help him. Because Alex listened to his parents, he understands the challenges that they have. Try to be a good listener next time a friend tells you about something they are excited about or a problem that they have. Also, try to be a good listener when talking with your parents.

Bodhi's Dad Offers To Help

The next day at Bodhi's house, Bodhi's dad hears about the problem that Alex's dad has. Bodhi's dad loves helping other people and offers to help. He tells Alex that he knows his dad is very talented at building things and offers to find him lots of work.

Bodhi's parents love to help other people because it makes them happy. When we help other people, they feel happy and we feel happy. Remember being happy is a big part of wellness. Maybe you could help your parents tonight by cleaning up your room. After you have done this, show your parents. They will be so surprised and happy. **How else could you help your parents?**

A Dream Come True

Alex's dad and Bodhi's dad meet at the Island Bookstore for coffee. Bodhi's dad explains that there is plenty of work to do on Paradise Key and that he will gladly hire Alex's dad to help. Alex's dad accepts his offer. He knows that this will really make Alex happy if they stay on the island. Bodhi and Alex overhear their conversation. Alex is going to get to stay on Paradise Key! This is truly a dream come true.

Alex is very grateful that his parents are allowing him to stay on Paradise Key with his new friends. He knows that his family will always be there for him. You will always be there for your parents too. Why don't you get some exercise with your family today, because you want them to be healthy too. You can go for a walk, kick the soccer ball, or work in the yard with them. Anything that gets your body moving.

The Exercise Station

Alex's dad does not waste any time getting to work. First, he builds a beautiful sign to mark the start of the trail that leads to the top of Mount Mango. He also builds an Exercise Station where Bodhi can do some pull ups while Izzy stretches. Even Sammy the squirrel wants in on the fun. If you take care of your body by exercising, it allows you to do fun things and enjoy this amazing planet.

Let's get some exercise. Let's get moving by doing 10 Jumping Jacks. Next, build your muscles by seeing how many push ups and how many sit ups that you can do. Finally, stretch your legs like Izzy is doing. Maybe your teacher can show you some other ways to stretch also.

The Meditation Station

Next, Alex's dad finds a beautiful spot on a hill overlooking the cove to build a Meditation Station. Izzy, Alex and Sammy take time for a quick meditation. All three of them find the sound of the rain very soothing.

Let's meditate with Izzy, Alex, and Sammy. Maybe your teacher or parents can put on some relaxing rain background sounds. Take some slow deep breaths and just chill for a while in Paradise Keys new Meditation Station. Try to meditate for 5 minutes. **Why do you think that meditation is good for your brain?**

The Juice Bar

Alex's dad's next project is a Juice Bar where the Wellness Crew can make healthy smoothies with the fruits they find on the island and some of the vegetables from Mother Nature's Garden. Remember fruits and vegetables have all of the nutrients that your body needs.

Ask your parents to take you to a local juice shop to try a healthy smoothie. You can also ask them to help you make a smoothie at home in the blender. Use frozen fruit to make your smoothie cold and smooth. **How did it taste? Did all of those healthy fruits and vegetables make you feel better?**

Sharing Their Wellness Secrets With Others

On page 42 of the workbook, Alex had a great idea. If they wrote their 7 secrets to wellness on each of the 7 buoys leading into the cove, then they would no longer be secrets. Everyone who came to the island would learn them, and then they too could live happy, healthy lives.

You are part of the Wellness Crew and they want you to paint one of the signs also. Which is your favorite wellness secret? The 7 secrets are written on page 41 of the workbook. Paint the sign for your favorite secret. **How can you share that secret with others?**

Mr. Bob's Printing Machine

The Wellness Crew has completed their book which explains their 7 secrets to wellness. They explain to Mr. Bob why they titled their book "The 7 Buoys." Remember from page 42 that the 7 Buoys leading into the cove keep boats on course. Likewise, the 7 wellness secrets, which they have now written on the 7 buoys, lead kids to a happy and healthy life. Mr. Bob is very impressed and tells them that he can print the books for them by the end of the week.

You have been working hard with the Wellness Crew. Now it's time to just relax and have fun. Put on some relaxing music, take your time, and color in Mr. Bob's Amazing Printing Press. **Why do you think it is important to take time to relax every day?**

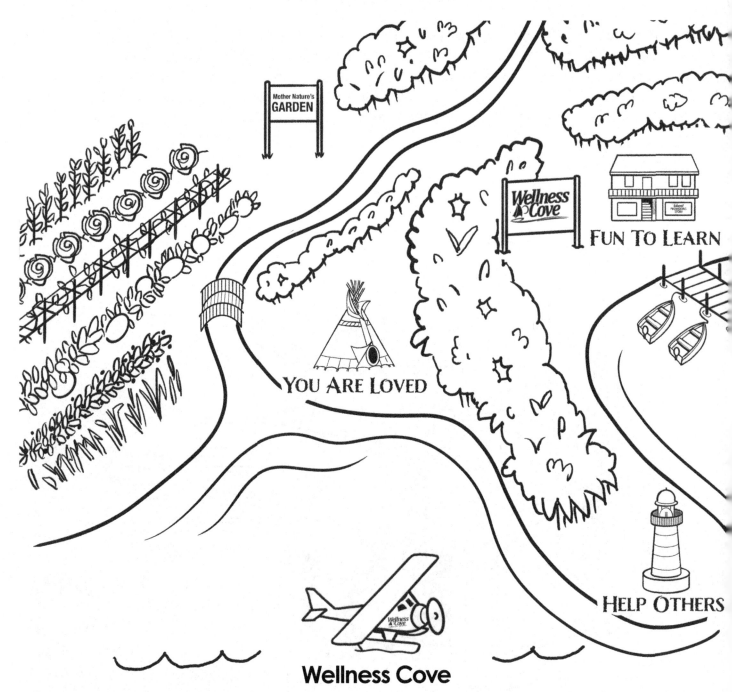

Wellness Cove

After dropping off their book "The 7 Buoys" for Mr. Bob to print, the Wellness Crew hikes back to the cove to chill. They climb to the top of the lighthouse. Looking out on the peaceful cove, they decide that it should be named Wellness Cove because this is a place where they will always be happy and healthy.

See if you can find the following things on the map.

1. Mother Nature's Teepee
2. Exercise Station
3. Meditation Station
4. Island Provisions Store
5. The Juice Bar
6. Alex's sailboat
7. Lighthouse

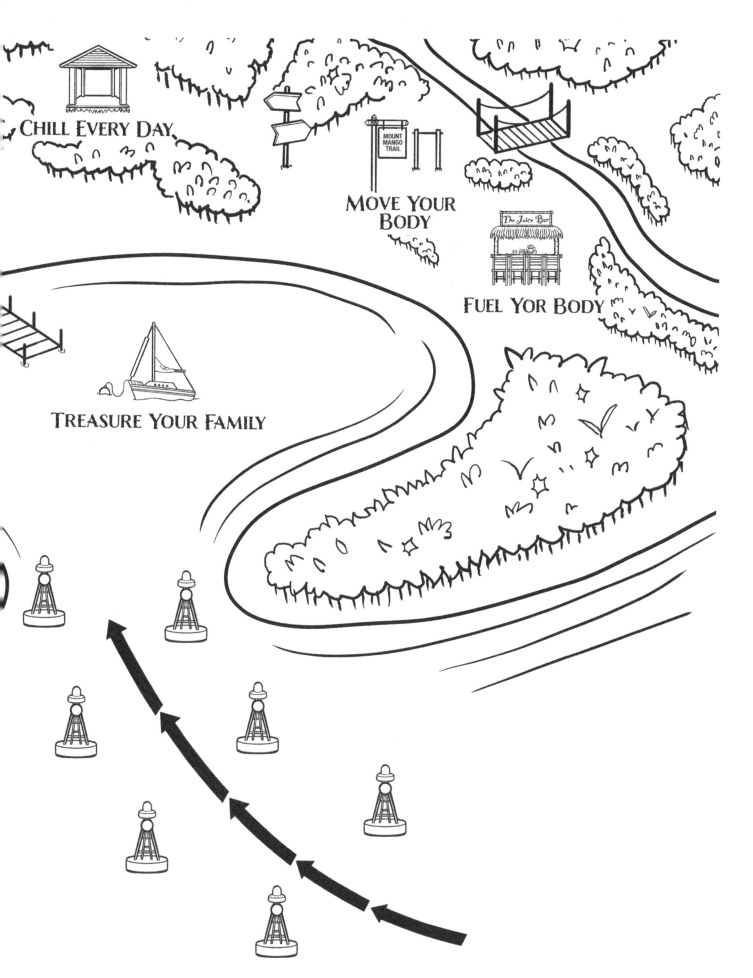

CHILL EVERY DAY

MOUNT MANGO TRAIL

MOVE YOUR BODY

The Juice Bar

FUEL YOR BODY

TREASURE YOUR FAMILY

Chapter 5
The 7 Buoys

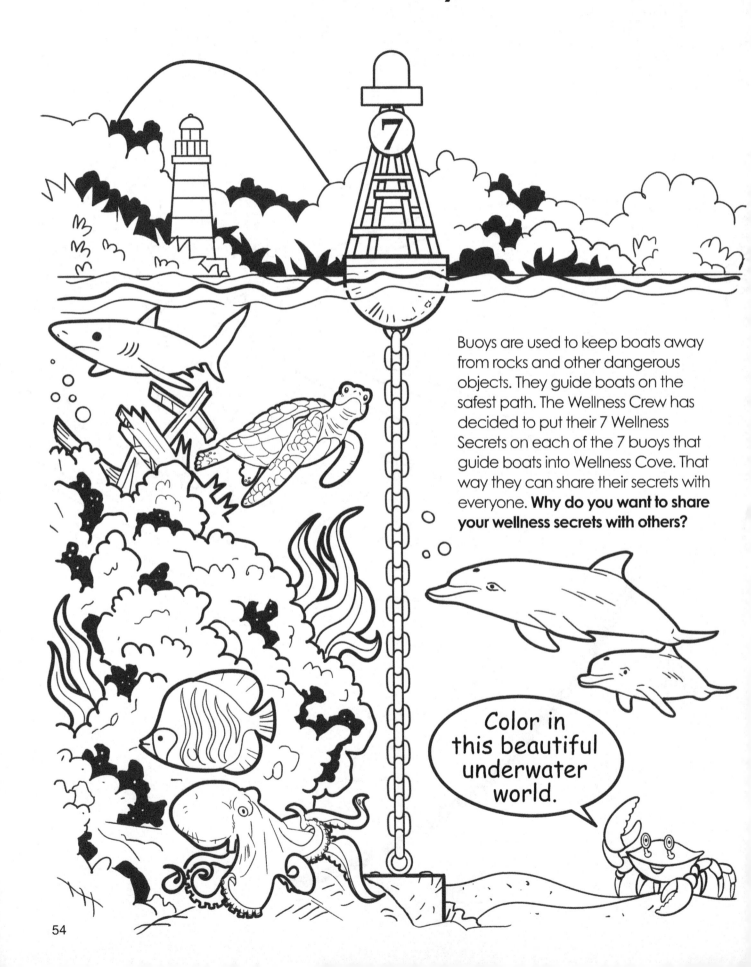

Buoys are used to keep boats away from rocks and other dangerous objects. They guide boats on the safest path. The Wellness Crew has decided to put their 7 Wellness Secrets on each of the 7 buoys that guide boats into Wellness Cove. That way they can share their secrets with everyone. **Why do you want to share your wellness secrets with others?**

Color in this beautiful underwater world.

Love yourself and love others exactly as they are. Don't change who you are to please others. You're fine just the way you are. You are not perfect, nobody is. If you make a mistake, that is ok, forgive yourself. At the same time, love others exactly as they are. If they make a mistake, forgive them.

Enjoy this amazing planet. We are blessed with a beautiful planet covered with mountains, oceans, waterfalls, and forests. Our planet is populated with all kinds of interesting animals, birds, and fish. Outside is the best place to exercise. Take care of your body by moving, using your muscles, and getting fresh air. Wellness is an adventure. With your friends, get outside and enjoy our beautiful planet. Be grateful for it and take care of it.

Chill every day. Life can get stressful. However, by taking the time to relax or meditate each day, you can learn to stay calm and set an example for others. You can be a peacemaker in this world. You can make this world a better, more peaceful, place.

You learned on page 20 that wellness means taking care of your body and brain. The best way to take care of your brain is to use it. And, when you use your brain, you realize that **it's fun to learn, and cool to be smart.** We are all smart in different ways. You are smart in your own unique way. Keep reading, and keep learning, because this world needs your ideas. You can make this world a better place.

Fuel your body with the nutrients that it needs. You have an amazing body and brain. Take care of them by fueling them with the nutrients that they need. Eat lots of plant foods like fruits, vegetables, beans, and nuts. Eat mindfully by slowing down and really enjoying your food.

Your family will always be there for you. Having someone to celebrate good times with, or talk to when things are not so good, is healthy. Just like us, our families are all very different. Just like us, our families are not perfect. However, our families are fine just the way they are. Be grateful for having a family that loves you and will always be there for you. **Treasure your family.**

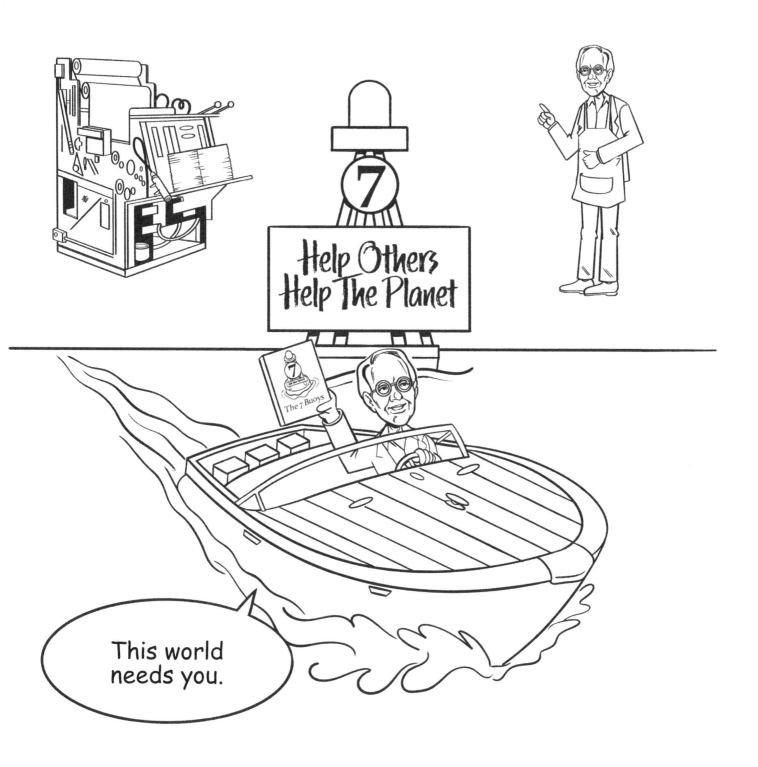

Help Others
Help The Planet

This world needs you.

You have learned on this journey that you are unique, and that you have many unique talents. **Use your talents to help others and to help the planet.** When you help other people, you realize that you really can make a difference in the world. You are not "just" a kid. When you help the planet, by picking up trash for example, you are setting an example for others. This world needs you!

All Kids Should Be Happy & Healthy

The Wellness Crew, by working together, have written their book *The 7 Buoys*. Mr. Bob was nice enough to print their book for them. Bodhi's parents are going to help the kids get their book into schools everywhere by taking them to other schools. That way all kids can learn to live a happy and healthy life.

Congratulations on being part of the Wellness Crew and using your talents to help write *The 7 Buoys*. Now it is time to get to work! Draw yourself into the picture and help the others load the seaplane with books so that they can be delivered to schools all over the Tradewind Keys. Your Wellness Adventure is just beginning!

Your Next Adventure!

The next day, Izzy is walking on the beach and finds a bottle washed up on shore with a map.

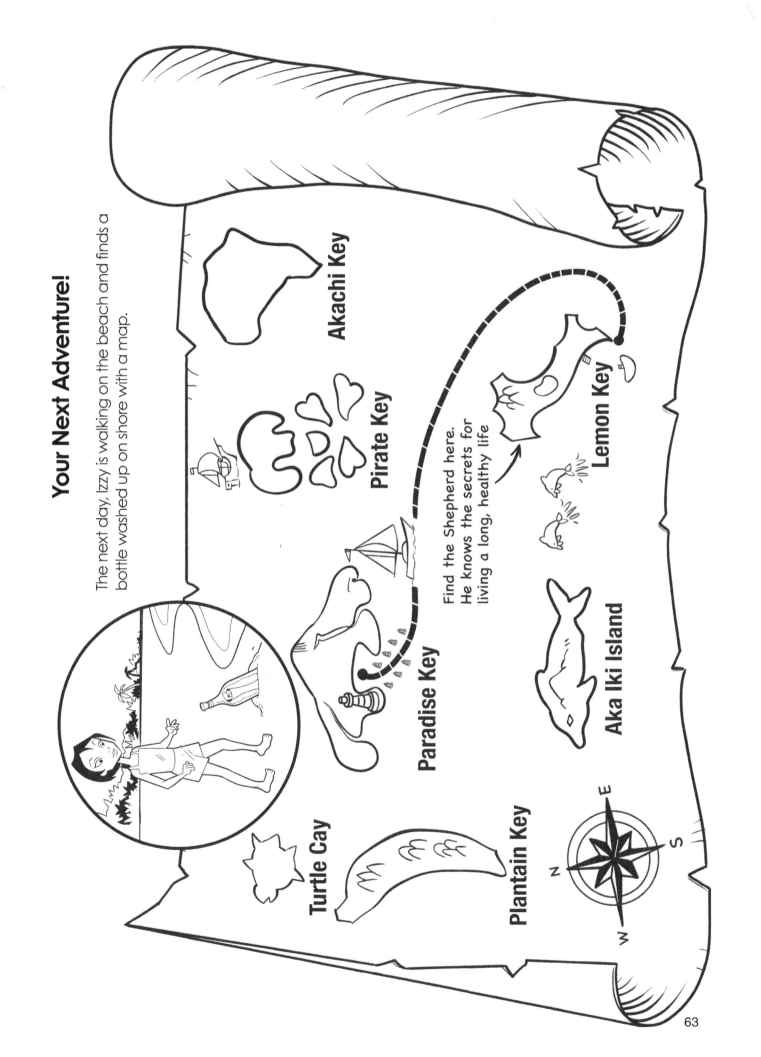

Akachi Key

Pirate Key

Turtle Cay

Paradise Key

Find the Shepherd here. He knows the secrets for living a long, healthy life

Lemon Key

Aka Iki Island

Plantain Key

TRADEWIND KEYS

Anguilla

British Virgin
Islands

Akachi
Key

Turtle Cay

Paradise Key

Pirate Key

Plantain Key

Lemon Key

Aka Iki Island

St. Croix

N
W   E
S

Made in United States
North Haven, CT
10 February 2023

32321805R00037